SAILING
LANGUAGE

SAILING LANGUAGE

The words sailors use, arranged so they can find the words they want for the particular use they want to make of them.

ELLIOTT DUNLAP SMITH

With Revisions and an Introduction

by

THOMAS R. MOORE

Drawings by Leslie S. Moore

SHERIDAN HOUSE

First published 2000 by
Sheridan House Inc.
145 Palisade Street
Dobbs Ferry, NY 10522

Copyright © 2000 by Sheridan House Inc.

A Cataloging-in-Publication record for this book is available from the
Library of Congress, Washington DC.

Designed by Jeremiah B. Lighter

Printed in the United States of America

ISBN 1-57409-117-4

ACKNOWLEDGEMENTS

*Special thanks to Marcia Chapman,
Captain Andy Chase and
the family of Elliott Dunlap Smith
for permission to republish* Yachting Language.

INTRODUCTION

ELLIOTT DUNLAP SMITH knew the right name for every knot, line, and fitting on his thirty-one-foot yawl, TEACHER'S PET, and his enthusiasm made it easy for me, an eager thirteen-year-old, to learn this new language. In the summer of 1954 he invited my uncle and me to cruise with him on TEACHER'S PET. From Sorrento, Maine, we sailed across Frenchman Bay, up Somes Sound, and spent the night at anchor in Somes Harbor near Acadia National Park. The next day we ran by Blue Hill's Long Island, tacked through Eggemoggin Reach, and spent the night at anchor in the Benjamin River. We sailed on as far as Buck Harbor. Those place names have stuck with me as tenaciously as the splices and knots Mr. Smith taught me: long splice, short splice, eye splice, back splice, bowline, clove hitch, reef knot, slip knot, rose, Turk's head, monkey's fist.

"Pull each strand out along the standing part of the line first and then pull it back," he said, showing me how to splice and then watching each attempt until I had it just right.

"This is how a captain in the German Navy taught me to tie a bowline," he said, "and it's far faster than the Boy Scout version with the tree and the rabbit. Lay the standing part over your left palm, then take the end and twist it through a loop on the line on your palm, finish it off—like this—and snug it. Now you do it. That's it. Now with your eyes closed. Good. Now behind your back."

He also knew the names of the spars, the sails, the rigging as well as the various orders for navigating and maneuvering the yawl. "Douse the mizzen," he said as we sailed in the capricious winds of Somes Sound, "and stand by to ease the jib sheet."

For Christmas that year I received an unexpected present: a copy of his little book, *Yachting Language,* inscribed "To my shipmate Tom Moore, from Elliott Dunlap Smith. Christmas 1954." It is a functional, precise compendium of, in Mr. Smith's words, "The words a yachtsman uses, arranged so he can find the word he wants for the particular use he wants to make of it." A slim, mimeographed book in a plastic spiral binding, it has been on my bookshelf for almost half a century now, keeping company with *The Ashley Book of Knots, Chapman's Piloting,* Duncan and Ware's *Cruising Guide to the New England Coast, The Lore of Ships,* and *American Practical Navigator.* I picture Mr. Smith in his Provost's office at the (then) Carnegie Institute of Technology in Pittsburgh refining his definitions between university duties. "Parcel," he writes, is to "wrap a rope in canvas to prevent chafing," followed by "Worm," to "wrap small stuff in the channel of the lay between strands so as to make a smooth tubular surface for parceling."

Although *Yachting Language*—now *Sailing Language*—was conceived in the era before fiberglass hulls, satellite-positioning systems, and gender-sensitive pronouns, the basic language remains the language of sailors today. The book draws on—and augments—a long tradition of sailing terms, and it continues to speak, with clarity and precision, to the sailor who wants to say it right. In his introduction to *The Elements of Style,* a somewhat more famous "little book" resurrected by E. B. White, White describes William Strunk, Jr.'s text as "a case for cleanliness, accuracy, and brevity in the use of English." Mr. Smith's book shoots for the same mark and it surely has earned another life as well.

THOMAS R. MOORE
Brooksville, Maine
September 2000

CONTENTS

III. The Sailboat Afloat   43

IV. Handling the Sailboat   53

Alphabetical Index of Terms   69

PART I

The Sailboat

QUALITIES OF A SAILBOAT

ABLE Competent and manageable in sailing under all conditions.
  Seakindly Pleasant to handle in a heavy sea.
  Seaworthy Able to survive winds and rough water.

BEAMY Broad in proportion to length.
  Flaring With sides rising outward.

BLUFF Perpendicular in lines, especially in the bow.

BRISTOL FASHION In excellent order.

BURDENSOME Capable of carrying a large cargo for the size of the craft.

FINE With slender fast lines, especially a sharp bow.

FULLY FOUND Completely equipped.

LOFTY With high masts and hence much "aloft."
  Top lofty Rigged too high for the hull.

OVERRIGGED Too heavy rigging (and too little sail area) for its size.

RAKISH Smart and saucy looking.
  With **raked masts** With masts slanting aft.

SMART Well kept and well handled.

SO SO Moderately well equipped.

STAUNCH Watertight and in seaworthy condition.

TENDER Quick to lean in a wind.
  Cranky Uncertainly and unpleasantly tender.
  Stiff Not leaning easily in a wind. The opposite of
    tender.

WEATHER HELM Tending to come into the wind as she
  leans.
  Ardent With excessive weather helm.
  Lee helm Tending to fall off as she leans.

WINDAGE, TO HAVE LITTLE (OR MUCH) To offer little (or
  much) resistance to the wind from rigging, fixtures,
  etc.

HULL (Types)

DISPLACEMENT HULL A hull that displaces a volume of
  water equal to the vessel's weight both at rest and
  underway.

PLANING HULL A hull designed to ride on the water's surface as the speed increases. Most sailboats have
  displacement hulls.

MULTIHULL VESSELS
  Catamaran Two hulls connected with a rigid trans-
    verse frame upon which the mast is stepped.
  Trimaran One central hull flanked by two smaller
    hulls.

HULL (Exterior)

AMIDSHIPS The part of the hull midway between stem
  and stern.

Bilge or **bilges** The hull between keel and waterline; also, the deepest void of the inside hull along the keel. *Bilge water* is leakage that collects there.
Waist The deck amidships.

BOW, BOWS, OR HEAD The forward part of the hull.
    Cutwater The visible exterior of the stem, especially near the waterline.
    Eyes The foremost part of the prow.
    Forefoot The part of the bow that lies in the water.
    Foresheets The part of the boat forward of foremast.
    Prow or **nose** The part of the bow which extends above the water.
    Stem The foremost timber forming the end of the bow.

BRIGHTWORK Any part of the hull or its fixtures that is varnished or made of polished metal.

DECK The floor-like surface at the top of the hull.
    Camber Transverse convex curvature of the deck.
    Cockpit A sunken part in the afterdeck for the helmsman and others to sit in.
    Gangway Any passageway on the deck, especially along the side of the cabin, or the narrow platform that spans from dock to deck.
    Rail A ridge along the outer edge of the deck.
        Bulwarks A high, sturdy rail.
        Coaming A high rail on the deck to shed surface water from the cockpit.
        Scuppers Drain holes through the rail or bulwarks.
        Taffrail The stern rail.
        Toe rail Narrow strip running on top of the gunwale.
    Sheer The fore-and-aft upturn of the deck.
        Sheer-line The profile of the bulwarks or rail as seen from abeam.

OVERHANG The part of the bow or stern which protrudes out over the water.

SKIN The entire exterior surface of the hull.

STERN The after-part of the hull.
  Counter The stern-deck.
  Fantail A rounded, fan-shaped, overhanging stern with no transom.
  Quarter The sailboat's hull between abeam and dead astern.
  Transom The sternboard of a flat-sterned boat.

TOPSIDES The portion of the exterior hull between the waterline and the rail.
  Boot top A stripe painted at the waterline.
  Freeboard The height of the topsides.
  Gunwale The strip of planking or the welt that runs along the upper edge of the topsides of a sailboat, or the upper edge of a small open boat. On an open boat gunwales may be open or closed by a strip called a *capping*. On a sailboat they are covered by a *covering board*, a wide deck edging inside of which the narrower deck planking begins.
  Tumblehome An inward turn of the topsides as they rise.

WATERLINE The line that the surface of the water makes or will make along the hull when the ship is afloat and in trim.

HULL (Interior)

BUNK OR BERTH Built-in sleeping units or beds.

BULKHEAD Vertical interior partition.

CABIN The living quarters of the vessel.
   Cuddy A small cabin.

FORECASTLE Storage space or sleeping quarters for the crew, generally in the bow.

GALLEY The kitchen.
   Charlie Noble The galley stove pipe.
   Chow Food.
   Mess A meal, or the place where meals are served.

HEAD The toilet.

HOLD The cargo space of the vessel, if any.

OVERHEAD The ceiling.

SOLE The floor of the cockpit or cabin.

STATEROOM Any partitioned-off sleeping quarters for owner or guests.

STOWAGE SPACE Storage space.
   Lazarettes Stowage compartments in the stern of a vessel.
   Lockers Stowage compartments.
   Racks Open stowage shelves.

TRUNK That part of the cabin raised above the deck.

Doghouse A small unit of the trunk over the hatchway and higher than the rest.

HULL (Openings)

HATCH, HATCHWAY, OR SCUTTLE A large opening through the deck for entering or loading the vessel.
Companionway A hatchway with an accommodation ladder or steps.
Hatch cover The cover over a hatch.
Hood A sliding hatchcover over a companionway.
Skylight A hatchcover set with glass or plastic.
Manhole A round, man-sized hatchway.

PORTS OR VENTS Small round openings through the deck or topsides, such as *hawseholes* for the anchor chain or rode, or *anchor ports*; *portholes* (round windows); and *mast holes*. A vent is often protected or extended by a *cowl* or metal hood.

HULL (Construction)

DIMENSIONS
Beam Greatest width.
Deadrise Angle of sidewise lift of the ship's bottom at the keel.
Draft Depth from waterline to lowest point on the keel.
Headroom Height of lowest overhead beams from the sole.
Length overall Stem to stern length as distinguished from length at the waterline.
Scantlings Dimensions of timbers.

MATERIALS (Fiberglass construction)

Fiberglass Polyester resin reinforced with glass fibers, sometimes molded around a balsa or foamed plastic core, with transverse bulkheads serving as structural components and with a hard exterior surface called the *gelcoat.*

MATERIALS (Wood construction)
Beams Horizontal thwartship timbers that support flooring or deck.
    Frames or ribs Thwartship beams rising from the keel to the deck and supporting the planking.
    Thwarts Large horizontal thwartship timbers.
Bulkhead Any upright partition; usually a thwartship division of the hull.
Carlings Fore-and-aft braces between deck beams.
Carvel-built Built with smooth-sided planking.
Clinker or **lapstraked** Built with each upper strake overlapping the one below it.
Cradle A temporary rack used to hold a vessel steady while it is being hauled out or stored.
Deadwood A vertical triangular plank on the inner side at the end of the keel, bracing its joint with a stem or sternpost, or at the end of the propeller shaft.
Floorboards Interior planks for walking upon.
Footlings Floor planks that rest directly on the ribs.
Forms or **molds** Braces to hold the ribs or planks during construction; also vernacular for "ribs."
Keel The main central fore-and-aft timber to which the frames are attached.
    Bilgeboards Boards similar to a centerboard placed in the bilges instead of the keel.
    Centerboard A vertical board passing through the keel amidships, adjusted so it can be lowered into the water from its after end and serve as a fin keel.
    Centerboard box A waterproof box built on the keel

into which the centerboard is hauled up when not in use.

False keel A central fin protruding down from the keel.

Fin keel A thin, deep false keel.

Keelson A fore-and-aft timber laid over the keel to brace it and usually supporting the floor timbers.

Leeboards Fins protruding down from the sides of a flat-bottomed vessel.

Knees Angular braces.

Limber holes Fore-and-aft drain holes through frames, floor beams, bulkheads, etc.

Planking or **planks** Any covering boards, especially those covering the ribs.

Strake A line of plank from stem to stern.

Garboard strake The plank nearest to the keel.

Shear strake The plank nearest to the deck.

Wales Strakes or protecting welts from stem to stern on the topside only.

Rudder The steering unit which is outside the ship.

Rudder port The vertical tube carrying the rudder post.

Rudder post The shaft to which the rudder is attached and by which it is turned.

Seams The joints between planks. They are *caulked* with cotton or *oakum* to make them watertight, and *payed* with putty to make the vessel's skin smooth.

Skeg A fin protruding from the after part of the keel, usually to protect the rudder and propeller.

Stanchions Upright bars or posts, such as support the deck or lifelines.

Stem The foremost timber of the hull extending from keel to deck at the prow.

Sternpost The aft timber attached to the end of the

keel. It is similar to the stem in double-ended vessels, and attached to the transom in flat-sterned vessels.

Stocks The supports holding a vessel while it is being built.

Stringers Fore-and-aft strips attached to and strengthening deck beams or frames on their inner side.

Timbers Any construction members used for strength.

SPARS

BOOM Any horizontal spar on a vessel, but especially the spar on the foot of a fore-and-aft sail, or a cargo-lifting spar rigged to the base of the mast.

Club A small boom.

Jib boom A spar to extend the bowsprit.

BOOMKIN A short stern sprit, such as is used to trim the jigger on a yawl.

BOWSPRIT A fixed spar running nearly horizontally out from the bow so as to make possible larger or more headsails. (If a bowsprit boom or club is set at an angle upward greater than the shear of the deck, it is *canted* or *steeved*.)

GAFF The spar at the top edge of a fore-and-aft sail.

Parts of a boom or gaff *Shaft, jaws* or *gooseneck* (attachment to mast).

MASTS

Parts of a mast (listed from the bottom up)

Heel, shaft, crosstrees (meeting of mast and spreaders), *masthead*.

Types *Foremast* The foremost mast.

>*Jigger or spanker mast*   A small mizzenmast stepped aft of the rudder post.
>
>*Mainmast*   The tallest mast.
>
>*Mizzenmast*   A mast aft of the mainmast.
>
>*Raked mast*   A mast that slants aft.

SPRIT   The spar running diagonally across and supporting the peak of a spritsail.

WHISKER POLE   A light jury spar to hold the jib out when running free.

YARDS   Horizontal spars that carry the sails of a square-rigger. *To cant yards* is to set them at an angle. *To cockbill yards* is to set the different yards at reverse angles.

SAILS (Types)

WORKING SAILS   The principal sail on each mast is called by the name of the mast: *mainsail, foresail, mizzen,* and *jigger.*

>**Headsails**   Staysails set on the stay of the mast, and forward of it. They are named, starting with the one nearest the mast, moving forward: *forestaysail, jib, flying jib,* and *jib topsail.*
>
>**Staysails**   Sails set on a stay and not on a mast.
>
>**Topsails**   Sails set above the principal sail, and called by the name of the mast; e.g., *foretopsail.*

LIGHT SAILS   Extra sails made of light cloth and only set in light airs or in races.

>**Balloon jib**   A large light sail set on the forestay that bellies out to catch the wind when quartering.

Drifter A light air sail for reaching or set to leeward with another jib to weather.

Genoa or **reaching jib** A large, flat, light sail, used in reaching, set on the forestay and extending aft of the shroud.

Spinnaker A light sail, not running on a stay, set opposite to or in front of the mainsail when running free.

SPECIAL TYPES OF SAILS

Fore-and-aft sail A sail with tack amidships and trimmed alee.

Gollywobbler A large quadrilateral sail that extends forward of the foremast and aft of the mainmast of a schooner and is flown in a reaching wind.

Lateen sail A triangular loose-footed sail, bent on a long yard, extending from the tack to the peak and hauled to the mast by a single halyard attached near its middle.

Loose-footed sail Sail not seized down to a boom along the foot.

Lugsail A quadrilateral fore-and-aft sail bent to a yard which is raised obliquely by a single halyard inside its end and without mast hoops or boom.

Marconi sail, jib-head sail, or **Bermuda rig** A very high-peaked triangular sail. It was developed from the American *leg-of-mutton* (broad triangular sail) but because the intricate wire stays needed to support the very lofty masts looked like the radio transmitting masts of the time, it was named for Marconi, the radio pioneer.

Spritsail A quadrilateral sail without gaff or boom, with its luff bent on the mast and its peak supported by a sprit running up to it from low on the mast.

Square sail A quadrilateral sail that is bent to a yard attached at its middle to the mast.

Storm canvas Sails of curtailed size and exceptionally heavy canvas used to ride out a storm.

Storm trysail A triangular storm sail rigged without unbending the working sails.

SAILS (Rigs)

FORE-AND-AFT RIGS

One masters

Catboat or *cat* One mast and mainsail but no headsails.

Cutter A sloop, the mast of which is stepped well aft, and usually with two headsails. Formerly, and still commonly in England, a sailboat is not called a cutter unless it has a perpendicular "cutter bow" and a large bowsprit.

Knockabout A small, day-sailing, sloop-rigged vessel with no bowsprit.

Sloop Headsails and mainsail.

Two masters

Double cat Two masts and no headsails.

Ketch Headsails, a mainsail, and a mizzen. The mizzenmast is forward of the helm.

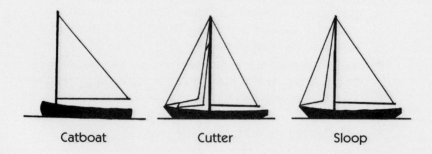

Catboat   Cutter   Sloop

Pinkie or *Pink* A blunt-bowed, double-ended ketch with outboard rudder, high, narrow stern, and stern bulwarks that extend aft of the rudder and above the tiller.

Schooner Headsails, a foresail, and a mainsail.

Yawl Headsails, large mainsail, and a small spanker or jigger, stepped aft of the helm.

Lugger Any fore-and-aft rig with lugsails.

SQUARE RIGS

Full-rigged ship Three or more masts, all square-rigged, plus a spanker on the mizzenmast.

Bark (or barque) Three or more masts, two square-rigged and one fore-and-aft rigged.

Barkentine Three masts, one square-rigged and two fore-and-aft rigged.

Brig Two masts, both square-rigged.

Brigantine Two or more masts, the foremast square-rigged and the mainmast carrying a fore-and-aft sail in place of a square mainsail.

Hermaphrodite brig Two masts, the foremast square-rigged and the mainmast fore-and-aft rigged.

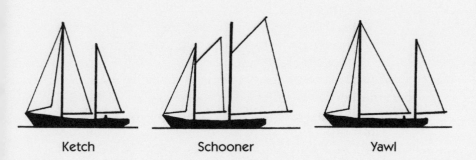

Ketch   Schooner   Yawl

SAILS (Parts)

THE BODY OF A SAIL
Belly The bulge in the body of the sail.

THE CORNERS OF A SAIL
Clew The lower outside corner.
Head The top of a triangular sail.
Peak The top corner of a gaff-headed or lateen sail, or the outer corner of a spritsail.
Throat The corner where the gaff meets the mast.
Tack The lower forward corner.

THE EDGES OF A SAIL
Foot Bottom.
Head Top.
Leech Outer edge.
Luff The edge along a mast or stay.
Roach The convex curve which a sailmaker puts in the edges of a sail to make the proper belly when the sail is filled.
Roached With outward curving leech.

THE FITTINGS OF A SAIL
Battens Wooden or fiberglass slats fitted into pockets in the leech of a sail to hold it flat.
Bolt rope A rope sewed to any edge of a sail to give it strength.
Tabling The hem of a sail at any edge to which a bolt rope is sewn, or multiple layers of reinforcing at corners.
Cringles Large metal eyelets in a sail as at the clew.
Grommets Small stitched or metal eyelets in a sail.
Reef points A series of short lengths of cordage sewed into grommets so as to extend on each side of the sail in a line parallel to the boom to secure the unused part of the sail when reefing.

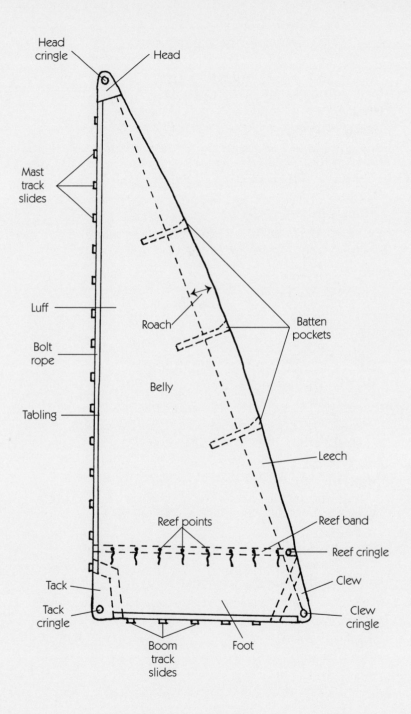

Reef band A strip of canvas that runs across the sail to strengthen it at the reef points.

THE CUT OF A SAIL Its shape and construction.
Sails are **long cut, cross cut,** or **mitred,** depending upon whether the seams run parallel to the leech, parallel to the foot of the sail, or parallel to the leech in the upper half and to the foot in the lower half.

SAIL MATERIAL Most working sails are made of *Dacron*; most light sails from *nylon.*

FLAGS

BURGEE A swallow-tailed or triangular yacht club or private signal.

THE COLORS *The national ensign* or the *national yacht ensign* (in the U.S., the national flag with thirteen stars in a circle and an anchor inside) constitute the ship's colors. No other flags do.

MEALS, OWNER ABOARD, etc., **flags** are "flags."

PENNANT A streamer or triangular flag.

UNION JACK Stars in a blue field (the "union" of the national ensign).
All flags are *hoisted* and *flown.*

RIGGING

RUNNING RIGGING Movable wire or rope, usually running through set blocks and other tackle that enable it to control the sails, spars, etc.

Cable Any heavy line, especially one used in docking, mooring, or anchoring.

Downhaul A line for dousing a sail.

Guy An auxiliary line used in trimming sail, etc.

Gilguy A guy to quiet slack halyards.

Halyard A line for raising and lowering a sail.

Lazy jacks A harness made of lines running from the topping lift to the boom to keep the sail in hand when it is lowered.

Leader Any line not a sheet for trimming a sail, such as a spinnaker leader.

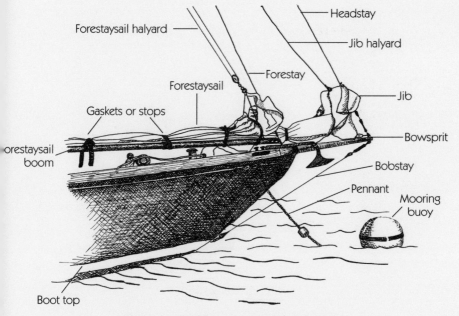

Bow of a traditional wooden schooner

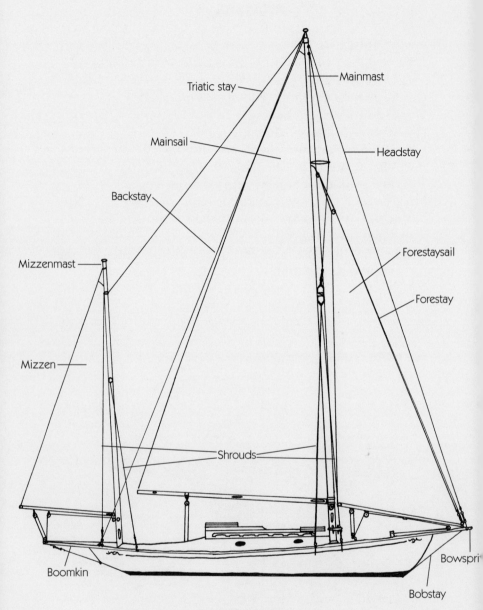

Traditional yawl

Line Any working rope on a vessel.

Outhaul A line rigged on the boom to pull the foot of a sail taut.

Preventer A line used to keep a sail from lifting its boom, or to check temporarily an undesirable movement of any running rigging or sail.

Sheet A line for trimming a sail. It is attached to the clew, or to a boom near the clew.

Topping lift A line that carries the weight of the boom when the sail is lowered.

STANDING RIGGING Fixed wire or rope bracings.

Backstay Any stay running aft.

Bobstay A stay under the bowsprit.

Forestay The stay running from the stem to a point below the masthead.

Headstay A stay running from the stem or bowsprit to the masthead.

Martingale The stay that passes over the end of the dolphin-striker under the bowsprit.

Shrouds Athwartship mast stays to provide lateral support.

Triatic stay A stay leading from the topmast head to the masthead next forward on a schooner, or, on a yawl or ketch, the stay leading from the main mast-head to the mizzenmast.

Whisker stays The horizontal side stays on the bowsprit of large vessels.

JURY RIG Any temporary device set up to take care of an emergency.

MISCELLANEOUS ROPES AND TIES

Earing A short piece of line seized to or spliced into a cringle, such as the "reef earings" at the leech of a line of reef points.

Gaskets (sometimes called *stops*) Strips of canvas, rope, or nylon used to furl a sail.

Heaving line A coil of line weighted on one end for heaving ashore or to another craft.

Lanyard A light line made fast to an article to secure it; e.g., a knife lanyard.

Lifeline A line rigged to prevent people from falling overboard.

Painter A docking or towing line.

Pennant (or **pendant**) A short light line attached to a spar or cable and usually ending in a block, thimble, or buoy.

Stops Threads confining a light sail so it will not fill while being set, or (loosely) gaskets.

FITTINGS

BINNACLE A stand for the compass, with a lighting device.

BITTS A heavy, short standing post or posts for belaying or snubbing cable.

BOLLARD A single bitt.

CHOCK A guide at the rail or bowsprit for the painter or anchor cable.

DAVITS Tackle for hoisting and carrying a dinghy or lifeboat onboard.

DECK FITTINGS
  Deck block A block attached to the deck.
  Deck bolts Screws or bolts fixed to the deck, such as *screw eyes, eye bolts,* and *ring bolts.*

Deck plate Any flat metal fixture on a deck, especially a small metal port with a flat, metal, screw-in cover.

Fairlead A guide for running rigging screwed to the deck and usually without a sheave.

Runner A track running along the side of the deck. It usually carries a slide to which a backstay is bent, and is used to set the backstay quickly.

HULL FITTINGS

Chain plate A metal strip on the topside of the hull, which serves as a footing for the shrouds. It runs from the gunwale to the waterline.

Gudgeons and **pintles** Eyebolts and pins that support the rudder.

Seacock A pipe, with a valve, opening through the hull into the sea.

LOGGER HEAD Bitts at the bow or stern that descend to the keel for bracing.

ROLLER-FURLING SYSTEM A mechanism that furls a sail by rolling it around a boom or a stay

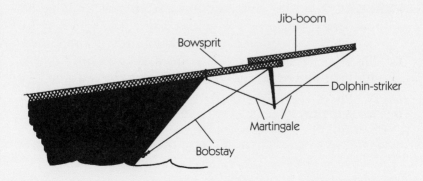

RUNNING LIGHTS and **RIDING LIGHTS** Lights on the stays or masts used to warn other boats when running or when riding at anchor at night.

SPAR FITTINGS
    Boom traveler A metal bridge on a boom with a traveling ring to which a sheet block is attached.
    Bridle A wire rope sling on a gaff or boom to carry a traveling block and distribute the strain.
    Dolphin-striker A metal strut running down from the bowsprit.
    Mast coat or **boot** A canvas coat going around the mast near the deck and over onto the deck, to keep water from leaking through the masthole.
    Struts or **spreaders** Braces at right angles to the mast to spread shrouds or stays.
    Tang A metal ferrule or plate on a spar with rings to attach rigging to.
    Track A rail attached to a spar on which run the slides that hold the edges of the sail.
    Truck A cap on the top of the mast, usually fitted with sheaves for flag halyards.

STANCHION A standing post.

TRAVELER A bridge running athwartship and attached to the deck, made of a steel bar and carrying a ring to which the sheet block is shackled, thus enabling this block to "travel" across the deck as the vessel tacks, and the sail to be sheeted down from the lee side. On commercial ships the bar is sometimes called a *deck horse* and the ring, a "traveler."

TURNBUCKLE A screw device to take up on a stay.

WINCH A drum and ratchet with a lever for increasing the pull in any hauling.

Capstan A very large vertical-drum winch.

Parts of a winch *Handle, drum, ratchet,* and *pawl* (which drops into the ratchet to prevent it from turning back).

Windlass A large horizontal-drum winch.

TACKLE

BLOCKS, CLEATS, etc.

Belaying pins Removable, longheaded metal pins that fit in holes in a *pin rail* and are used for belaying halyards.

Blocks The sea word for pulleys that are encased in a shell. The parts of a block are the *shell* in which the grooved wheel, the *sheave*, rotates on the *pin* between two *cheeks*. Between the sheave and the top of the shell is the *swallow* through which the line is reeved. Sometimes simple sheaves are mounted in a slot in a spar.

Bullet block Small metal block with one ring.

Cheek block A block screwed flat to a spar.

Cleats Two-armed belaying fixtures.

Snatch block A block with an opening on one side through which the line can be rigged into the block without reeving it through the swallow. Blocks may have a *shackle*, a *thimble*, a *becket* (a ring at the bottom as well as top), be a *bridle block* or be double (with two sheaves).

BLOCK AND TACKLE Rope and blocks reeved ready for use.

Purchase (or **handy Billy**) A movable block and tackle consisting of rope and two blocks, at least one of which is double.

Jig or *jigger* Any temporary device, such as a purchase, that helps get a particular job done. Sometimes called a rig, though rigging is properly more permanent.

CORDAGE *(All working ropes on a vessel are referred to as lines.)*

Kinds of cordage (roughly in descending scale of size) *Cable* (may be chain), *rope, line, cord, marline (tarred), light stuff, twine, yarn.*

Fibers are twisted to make **yarns.**

Yarns are twisted to make **strands.**

Strands are twisted to make **rope.**

Ropes are twisted to make **cable.**

The parts of a line in use

Bitter end The inboard end of a cable or line.

Fall That part of a line between the user and the free end.

Hauling part That part of a line between the user and a block or other movable rigging.

Standing part That part of a line between the user and where it is made fast or coiled.

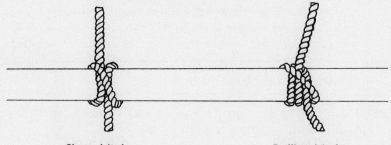

Clove hitch   Rolling hitch

Bends Knots by which one rope is secured to another, or to a bit of running gear. The most useful bends are the *fisherman's*, *sheet*, and *double-sheet*.

Square or reef knot

Bight A loop in a rope.

Chafing gear Wrapping to protect a rope from chafing.

Ends Ways of finishing the end of a rope, such as *crown*, *wall*, *whip*, and *rose*. A *cow-tail* is an unraveled rope end.

Bowline

Hitches Rope ties to bitts, cleats, and spars. The most useful hitches are *blackwall*, *clove*, *half*, *two halves*, *rolling*, and *timber*.

Irish pennant A rope end dangling from a spar or cleat, instead of being properly secured.

Knots The most useful knots are *bowline*, *bowline on bight*, *slip*, *square* or *reef*, and *leader*. For instructions as to how to tie these knots, and for information on the less common knots, see one of the books on knots.

Bowline on bight

A round turn A bend of rope that goes all the way around an object so that it overlaps itself rather than making a U-turn only.

Splices The joining of rope by interweaving the strands. The commonest splices are *eye*, *short*, *long*, and *end*.

Shackle and pin

Toggle A short stick spliced into a rope.

SMALL TACKLE

Shackle A metal horseshoe closed with a screw pin used for attaching chain, etc., to rings, etc.

Snaps, slides, and **mast hoops** Devices for attaching a sail to a stay or boom.

Thimble A tear-shaped metal lining for an eye splice.

Eye splice

GROUND AND DOCKING TACKLE
Anchors

Bower A large anchor carried in the bow.

Bruce A burying anchor originally developed for offshore drilling rigs.

CQR ("Secure") A plow anchor developed in England with a single fluke pivoting at the end of the shank.

Danforth An anchor with flukes pivoting on the stock at the end of the shank.

Grapple An anchor with four sharp prongs.

Kedge A light anchor used for kedging or warping.

Mooring A permanent anchoring unit consisting of a weight or permanent anchor such as a *mushroom*, a cable (the rode), and a buoyed pennant which the incoming vessel picks up.

Sea anchor A large ridged cone or other device towed overboard to check drift and hold the boat's head into the wind in a storm.

Sheet anchor A storm anchor carried below decks in the *foresheets*.

THE PARTS OF A DANFORTH ANCHOR

Becket The hole at the upper end of the shank.

Crown The lower end of the shank where it joins the stock.

Flukes The flat holding terminals of the anchor.

Head The upper end of the shank.

Palms The two flat surfaces on the crown opposing the planes of the flukes.

Shank The mainshaft.

Stock The crossbar passing through the crown.

CABLE The rope or chain attached to the anchor rings or mooring stone.
  Shot The length of cable equal to 15 fathoms (90 feet) in the United States and 12½ fathoms (75 feet) in Great Britain.

FENDERS Bumpers to prevent the topsides from coming into contact with a pier or another vessel.

PENNANT A light rope attaching the buoyed rode to the boat.

RODE That part of an anchor or mooring cable running from the boat or buoy to the bottom.

SCOPE The length of the rode. *To give more scope* is to pay out more cable.

WARP A cable used in pulling the vessel to a wharf, etc.

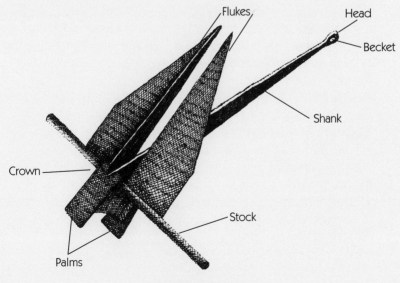

Danforth anchor

GEAR

NAVIGATING GEAR

Anemometer A device to measure wind velocity.

Compass An instrument for determining north.

Depthsounder An electronic device that measures depth.

GPS (Global Positioning System) An electronic device that receives satellite signals to determine position.

Lead A lead and line used to measure depth.

Log An instrument for determining the speed of the vessel through the water or the distance traveled.

LORAN (LOng RAnge Navigation) An electronic system using shore-based radio transmitters and receivers on board vessels in order to determine position.

Peloris An instrument for taking bearings from the vessel.

RADAR (RAdio Direction And Ranging) An electronic device to detect vessels and terrain in low visibility.

RDF (Radio Direction Finder) An electronic device to receive radio bearings in order to determine position.

Sextant An instrument for taking the "sights" on the sun, moon, or stars for celestial navigation.

VHF (Very High Frequency) A radio to communicate with other vessels or with shore transmitters.

SAFETY GEAR

EPIRB (Emergency Positioning Indicating Radio Beacon) A device to transmit an emergency signal on a preset frequency.

PFD (Personal Flotation Device) A lifejacket.

SHIP'S GEAR

Boat hook A free spar with a blunt hook in its end for catching hold of a wharf, boat, pennant, etc.

Bucket The sea name for a pail.

Gurry bucket A bucket for galley refuse.

Ditty bag or **box** A container for sail- or clothes-mending gear, such as sail needles, small line, thread, *sail hook* (a hook on a line that holds canvas so that the sailmaker can pull on it while sewing), and a *palm* (sailmaker's thimble).

Dodger A removable screen to protect the cockpit from wind and spray.

Lamps Lights used for illumination.

Lights Lights used to show where the ship is and is going.

Marlinspike A metal or wood spike used in splicing.

Shore A free spar used to brace or push.

Swab The sea name for a mop.

WORKING BOATS

MOTORBOAT OR LAUNCH A small harbor boat driven by power.

ROWBOATS

Dory A narrow-bottom, almost double-ended rowboat with high, flaring, flat sides, usually used for fishing.

Skiff Any harbor rowboat.

Tender Any boat towed or carried by a larger craft for harbor service.

Dinghy A round-sided, beamy, short tender with ample freeboard.

Pram A slab-sided, flat-bowed, beamy tender.

ROWBOAT GEAR

Rowlocks, oarlocks, or (on fishing rowboats) **thole pins** The braces for the oars while rowing.

Sculls or **oars** The means of propulsion. The parts of an oar are the *handle, loom, neck, blade,* and *tip.*

ROWBOAT PARTS

Chines The angles that are made by the meeting of the sides and bottom in flat-bottom or V-sided boats; also, lengthwise braces that run in the chines.

Foresheets The forward part of a boat.

Gunwales A wale at the top of the sides.

Stern sheets A seat running along the sides and across the transom at the stern.

Stretchers Bracers for the oarsman's feet.

Thwart Any cross seat or brace.

PART II

The World Around the Sailboat

LAND AND SEA

CHANNEL A safe, generally used passageway between un-derwater dangers, especially one entering a harbor.
Fairway A straight course down a channel.

GULF, ESTUARY, BAY, BIGHT, POND, COVE Indentations in the land, listed in order of declining size. Estuaries are river-mouth bays, bights are only slightly indented.

HARBOR A sheltered body of water suitable for an anchorage.
Dock A basin between *wharves* or *piers*, or, more com-monly, a pier or wharf.
Gunkhole A small casual harbor.
Roadstead A large, rather open harbor.

HOLDING GROUND The bottom in terms of anchorage.

LANDFALL The first sight of land after sailing out of sight of land.

OFF SOUNDINGS In water too deep for fathoming with a hand lead.

OUTLYING Far from shore.

REEF or SHOAL Rock or sand just above or below water level at low tide.
Bar A long, sandy shoal.

SEAWAY A stretch of open water with a heavy swell or sea.

SOUND, WAY, REACH Sheltered passageways open at both ends, listed in order of size. A reach usually runs across the prevailing wind so as to afford a reaching wind when sailing either way.

TIDE The twice daily fall and rise of the water level due to the attraction of the moon. Tides *flood, swell,* or *make* (rise) and *ebb* (fall); are at *high water* or *low water* at *the turn of the tide* from ebb to flood and flood to ebb respectively. There is *slack water* when the tide pauses or turns.

Current The running of water due to a tide or stream.
> *Eddy* A whirl or back motion in a tide current.
> *Tide race* An area of rapid tide current.
> *Tide rip* A contrasting line of waves or ripples due to the contact of two tide currents running in opposite directions.

Drift The speed in knots of a tide current.

Lee tide A tide that sets to leeward so that wind and tide current run together.

Range The difference in height between high and low water.

Set The direction of a tide current.

To set To flow in a direction or force a boat in a direction.

Spring and **neap tides** The semi-monthly tides with the highest and lowest ranges respectively.

Weather tide A tide that sets to windward.

TIDEWAY A stretch of water with a strong tide current.

WATER, BROKEN Water disturbed by current running over shoals or by the passage of a vessel.

Backwash The churning water driven astern by the propeller or against the boat when engines are reversed.

Bone in the teeth The foam at the bow of a fast-moving boat.

Wake The broken water and waves astern of a moving boat.

WAVES An undulation of the sea.
Breaker A wave that breaks on a shore or rock.
Crest and **trough** of waves Top and bottom.
Sea Wind-driven waves collectively.
  Chop An abrupt up-and-down or broken sea, usually due to the opposition of wind and current or two adverse currents.
  Following sea A sea running in the same direction as the vessel.
  Head sea A sea running head on to the vessel.
Spindrift The fine spray blown off the top of a wave by a strong wind.
Swell Waves not due to present wind.

WINDS AND WEATHER

BEAUFORT SCALE A wind scale that correlates sea conditions and wind speed from force 0 (calm) to force 12 (hurricane).

CALM, LIGHT AIR, BREEZE OR BREEZE OF WIND (gentle or light, moderate and fresh), **BLOW, GALE, STORM, HURRICANE** Descriptions of the air, listed in order of amount of its motion.

CATSPAW A patch of ripples caused on a calm sea by a puff.

CHANGES IN WIND
  To back To shift against the sun. *To haul* is sometimes used with this meaning. When wind is abeam, *to haul* is to shift forward, and *to veer* is to shift aft.

To blow over To stop blowing and clear (of a storm).
To drop To stop blowing.
To freshen, breeze up, or to **blow up** To grow stronger.
To moderate To drop somewhat.
To shift or haul To change direction.
To veer To shift with the sun (or clockwise).

FAIR WEATHER Sunny weather, usually includes good to moderate sea conditions.

FOUL WEATHER Rainy, foggy, cloudy, or squally weather.

HEAVY WEATHER A hard blow.

PUFFS, FLAWS, GUSTS, SQUALLS, CAP FULL OF WIND Small patches of wind, listed in order of their strength.

SLANT or **STRETCH OF WIND** A usable unit of wind.

SLICK A calm streak on rippled water.

SPANKING BREEZE or wind Desirably strong wind.

BEARINGS (Directions of objects or wind from the vessel)

BEARINGS (Compass)

POINTS The thirty-two divisions of the compass rose are listed below. Today, compass directions are usually given in degrees instead of points.
The cardinal points North, east, south, and west.
The angles between these points are quarters.

POINTS

North, north by east, north-northeast, northeast by north, northeast, northeast by east, east-northeast, east by north.

East, east by south, east-southeast, southeast by east, southeast, southeast by south, south-southeast, south by east.

South, south by west, south-southwest, southwest by south, southwest, southwest by west, west-southwest, west by south.

West, west by north, west-northwest, northwest by west, northwest, northwest by north, north-northwest, north by west.

One-quarter, one-half, three-quarters Fractions of a point in the direction from the full point indicated; e.g., NW ½ W, is one-half of a point west of northwest. The direction given is usually that of the last cardinal point included in the name of the point; e.g., S by W ¾ W instead of SSW ¼ S.

Due Exactly in a compass direction.

BEARINGS (Wind Directions)

Wind bearings may also be given in compass points or bearings from the vessel.

FAIR WIND or **FAVORING WIND** Any wind enabling one to hold a desired course whether close hauled or free.

FOLLOWING WIND A wind blowing from astern so that the boat is sailing free.

HEAD WIND A wind so nearly dead ahead that it is necessary to tack.

LEADING WIND A wind forward of abeam but not so nearly dead ahead as to require tacking.

ONSHORE and **OFFSHORE WIND** Blowing toward or away from the shore.

QUARTERING WIND A wind blowing from the quarter.

WIND ABEAM A wind that comes directly at right angles to the boat.

WIND BROAD OFF A wind somewhat abeam.

BEARINGS (In Relation to the Vessel)

Dead ahead, or **bow on**	000°	⎫
1, 2, 3, points on starboard bow		Ahead
Broad on starboard bow	045°	⎭

3, 2, 1, points forward of starboard beam		⎫
Broad on the starboard beam or broad abeam to starboard	090°	Abeam
1, 2, 3, points abaft the starboard beam		⎭

Broad on the starboard quarter	135°	⎫
3, 2, 1, points on the starboard quarter		Astern
Dead astern	180°	⎭

The bearings from the port side are similar.
Dead Directly.
Broad Squarely off.
Alongside Close to the vessel.

Abreast Alongside and abeam.

Ashore From the vessel to the shore.

Leeward Down the wind from the vessel.

Windward Into the wind from the vessel.

Windward or **leeward** (or **lee**) **shore** A shore to the windward or leeward of the vessel.

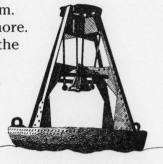

Bell buoy

AIDS TO NAVIGATION

BUOYS

Bell A buoy with a bell making a single tone.

Can An unlighted, odd-numbered, green, cylindrical buoy.

Gong A buoy with gongs making multiple tones.

Nun An unlighted, even-numbered, red, cylindrical buoy with a cone-shaped top. Red buoys should be left to starboard on entering a harbor, green left to port. *Memory device* Red-Right-Returning.

Whistle A buoy with a whistle or horn sounded by sea motion.

Can buoy

DAYBEACON An unlighted marker on land or a submerged shoal.

RANGE Two beacons placed so that when sighted in line they give an exact bearing.

Nun buoy

RULES OF THE ROAD Navigational safety regulations regarding movement and identification of vessels.

SAFE WATERMARKS Are used to mark fairways, mid-channels and offshore approach points.

PART III

The Sailboat Afloat

THE SAILBOAT AT REST

TO BE AFLOAT To ride on the water without touching bottom.

TO BE IN TRIM To be properly balanced by ballast and load.
 Out of trim Badly balanced.
  By the head (or *stern*) Trimmed so as to lie too low in the bow or stern.
 To be on an even keel To have no list or heel.
 To list or **to have a list** To be tipped to starboard or port because poorly trimmed.

TO BE AT ANCHOR OR MOORING To be secured by a cable running to an anchor or fixed mooring. Vessels *ride* or *lie* at anchor or mooring in their *berth*. When at anchor, they *tail* away from the anchor. If they tail down the wind, they are *wind rode*. If down the tide, they are *tide rode*. They *ride out* a storm if they stay at anchor or are *hove to* until the storm abates. Anchors take or *bite* when they cut into the bottom.
 To dock To come alongside a dock and come to rest.
 To drop anchor To anchor.
 To kedge To warp a vessel by carrying a small anchor ahead and hauling the vessel up to it. Usually this is done to pull a vessel over a bar; or in a calm or in narrow waters, to move it against the tide current.
 To warp To pull a vessel by means of cables, as warping it into dock.

THE SAILBOAT UNDER SAIL

CONDITIONS AND WAYS OF SAILING

To be becalmed To have no wind.

To be under a press of sail or **to have crowded on sail** To be carrying more sail than is safe with the amount of wind that is blowing.

To be under full sail To have all regular sails set.

To be underway To have started sailing.

To bowl along To sail fast and merrily.

To careen To lean far over.

To coast To sail along the coast.

To cruise To sail for pleasure.

To draw (said of sails) To fill with wind so as to drive the vessel.

To foot To make good headway, especially in relation to the wind.

To get underway or **away** To start sailing.

To ghost To sail along when there is no apparent wind.

To have headway or **steerageway** To be moving fast enough to steer.

To lean To tip from the force of the wind.

To make sail To set the sails.

To set sail To put out from port.

To slat or slat about To roll in a calm and swell so that the sails flap and jerk.

WAYS OF SAILING, IN RELATION TO THE WIND

To be in stays or **in irons** To be brought to a stop dead into the wind so as to lose steerage way.

To beat or **tack** To sail to windward by changing back and forth from starboard and port tacks.

Hitch, leg, or *tack* To run on one tack while beating.

To come about To head into the wind and fill away on the other tack.

To forereach To turn into the wind and barge ahead from the vessel's momentum.

To make to windward To gain against the wind.

> *To claw* To make to windward with difficulty, especially offshore.

To misstay To get caught in irons when coming about.

To quarter To sail with wind on the quarter.

To reach To sail between close hauled and quartering.

> *A broad reach* A course with the wind between the quarter and abeam.
>
> *A close reach* A course with the sails nearly or actually close hauled but not involving beating.

To sail close hauled, by the wind, or **on the wind** To sail as close into the wind as possible.

> *To drive* To sail close hauled with the wind well into the sails.
>
> *Full and by* Close hauled and drawing well.
>
> *To pinch* To sail closer into the wind than is efficient.
>
> *To sail fine* To sail close hauled just short of pinching.
>
> *Strapped down* Close hauled, hard driven, and leaning.

To sail free To sail with the wind abaft abeam.

> *To be by the lee* To sail with the wind somewhat on the same side as the mainsail and thus be in danger of jibing.
>
> *To run* To sail *before, down,* or *off the wind,* or with *wind astern.*
>
> *To sail wing-and-wing* To run with one sail on each side.

To sail off and on To beat along a shore.

To sail off the wind To sail with the wind abeam to off the quarter.

> *To sail broad off* To sail with the wind abeam.

To sail large   To sail with the wind somewhat abeam.

CONDITIONS OF SAILING, IN RELATION TO LAND OR MARKS

Bound for   Sailing toward, as a goal, regardless of the immediate course.

To fetch, to make, or **to reach** a mark or point of land   To sail or be sailing so as to pass to windward of it without beating.

To **hail from** or **out of**   To sail from, as the vessel's home port.

To have leeway or **searoom**   To be far enough to windward of any obstacle or shore to be able to maneuver without risk of grounding.

Offing   The distance from shore.

To hug the shore   To keep close to it.

To make a course good   To reach a planned objective by the original course.

To pick up a mark   To sight it in a fog.

To round a mark   To fetch it and change course.

To sight a mark   To see it.

To weather or **to double** a mark or point   To leave it to leeward.

To *double a cape* is to round it in either direction.

WAYS OF SAILING, IN RELATION TO OTHER BOATS

To be alongside of a pier or vessel   To be at its side.

To be in collision with a vessel   To foul it badly.

To bear down on   To sail up to a vessel or mark from the windward.

To blanket another vessel   To sail too close windward of it so as to take its wind.

To foul a vessel or mark   To touch it while sailing.

To gain the wind of a vessel   To get to windward of it.

To give wide berth to   To keep well away from a vessel, buoy, or danger.

To outfoot another vessel To sail faster than it does.

To outpoint another vessel To sail closer into the wind than it does.

To overhaul a vessel To gain on it in a chase.

To overlap a vessel To have so far overtaken a vessel as to be unable to cross its stern without dropping back.

To overtake a vessel To catch up with it.

To sheer off To turn off one's course to prevent fouling.

To stand by another vessel To stay near it in order to help.

To stand in with another vessel To sail along with it.

THE SAILBOAT IN HEAVY WEATHER OR ADVERSE CONDITIONS

CAUGHT OUT Unexpectedly overtaken by foul weather at sea.

IN DISTRESS In any sort of difficulty.

TO BE BOWS UNDER To have the waves come over the bows.

TO BE SET To be carried to the lee or to the windward by the tide.

TO BE WINDBOUND or **WEATHER-BOUND** To be kept in port by weather conditions.

TO BROACH TO To slew so badly when running that the wind is broad abeam and the boat without headway.

TO DRIFT To move off course involuntarily due to current or wind.

Drift Rate of involuntary motion due to current or wind.

TO GROUND To run aground.

To be brought up To stop dead, because of grounding, or of having dropped anchor and overrun the anchor's scope.

To be high and dry To be aground so there is no water surrounding the vessel.

To be stranded To be stuck fast on the bottom, especially a beach.

To careen a vessel To tip it over on its sides, when grounded, in order to clean or paint its bottom.

TO HAVE SAILS ABACK, TO BE ABACK, or **TO BACK A SAIL** To have wind on the wrong side of a sail, so it flaps or fails to draw properly.

To be taken aback To become aback involuntarily.

TO HEADREACH To forge ahead when pointed into the wind.

TO HEEL, LAY OVER, or **LEAN** To tip in wind, or otherwise.

Angle of heel Amount of tip.

To be knocked down To heel until the sails are empty of wind and the ship is *on its beam ends.*

To capsize To tip over.

To careen To lean extensively.

Rail down Leaning so much the rail is awash.

TO JIBE To have the sails fill by the lee and come crashing over to the opposite side.

TO LABOR To go ahead with difficulty.

TO LIE TO or **HEAVE TO** To ride a blow at sea with sails and helm set in opposition so that the boat lies close to the wind but makes almost no headway.

TO MAKE HEAVY WEATHER OF IT To labor in a heavy wind or sea.

TO MAKE LEEWAY To drift or be driven down the wind.
Leeway Rate of wind drift.

TO PLOW To push along with an excessive *bone in the teeth* (i.e., white water at the bow).

TO RIDE A SEA EASILY or **HEAVILY** To go through it without or with difficulty and distress.

TO ROLL To tip from side to side due to the sea or swell.
To lurch To roll suddenly and heavily.
To pitch To tip in a fore-and-aft direction.
To pitchpole To tip stern over bow or bow over stern.
To plunge To pitch violently.
To pound To slap the waves with the bow when pitching.
To rock (said only of small boats) To be caused to tip from side to side by the movement of occupants.

TO SCUD To plow before a heavy wind under "bare poles" or almost no sail.

TO SLEW To swing involuntarily off the course.

TO SHIP WATER To take water into the cockpit or hull over the sides.
To be pooped To take in a wave over the stern when running.

TO TAKE A DUSTING To get soaked with spray in a squall.

TO SWAMP To fill with water.

> **To be awash** To be swamped and floating so low that the waves wash over the vessel.
>
> **To founder** To fill with water and sink.
>
> **To scuttle** To sink a boat deliberately.

TO YAW To swing involuntarily from side to side when running.

TROUBLE WITH GEAR

Ropes **foul,** or **kink,** instead of **running freely,** and if badly tangled become a **hurrah's nest.**

STANDING GEAR loosens and gets **slack,** and all gear when overslack has too much **play.**

Ropes and stays **part,** while fittings **give way.**

Anchors **foul** cables on the bottom, or **get fouled** by their cables or by the bottom.

Masts **work** and get loosened and when carried away the vessel is **dismasted.**

Decks and sides **stave in** or get **stove in** when they collapse from rot or get smashed by impact.

Gear of all forms gets **carried away** when it breaks or gets loose from its fittings so as to come free or **go overboard** or **get adrift.**

PART IV

Handling
the Sailboat

THE SHIP'S COMPANY

CAPTAIN The chief paid hand on a vessel.

CREW All on board who help to work on the vessel, except the skipper, whether guests or paid hands.

HELMSMAN The person who is steering.

LUBBER, GOONEY, or **GOON** An awkward member of the ship's company.

SAILOR, HAND, FORECASTLE HAND, PAID HAND, SQUARE-HEAD Hired sailor.

SEAMAN A person skilled in seamanship, the handling of a sailboat or ship.

SHIP'S COMPANY Everyone living on board the vessel.

SKIPPER The owner or person in command of the vessel. (The *Master* is the commander of a merchant vessel, and the *Captain* is the commander of a naval vessel. Both are addressed as Captain.)

WATCH The members of the crew on duty.

TERMS RELATING TO NAVIGATION

BEARING The direction of an object from the vessel.

COURSES Directions to the helmsman as to where to sail. Courses are *laid, plotted, set,* or *shaped. Charts,* not maps, are used.

DEAD RECKONING Finding position by speed, direction, and estimate of current rather than by fixes.

DEPARTURE The fix from which a course is plotted when leaving port (*taking a departure*).

POSITION or **FIX** of a vessel Its exact position determined by taking bearings or, when offshore, by sights on celestial bodies or by electronic means.

RUN The distance covered in a unit of time. It is *reckoned* or *calculated* in nautical miles (one minute of latitude, 6076 feet, or 1⅛ land miles). The speed of the run is measured in **knots**, i.e., sea miles per hour. To say "knots per hour" is thus always incorrect.

DIRECTIONS ON THE SAILBOAT

AFT, ABAFT, AFTER Toward the stern. (Never astern, which refers only to objects outside the vessel.)

ALOFT Up.

AMIDSHIPS In the middle of the vessel, especially with regard to length.

ATHWARTSHIP Across the vessel.

BELOW or **ALOW** Down. ("Below" is used for "below decks.")

FORWARD Toward the bow.

HAWSE The space between the bows and the anchor rode, when a ship is lying at anchor.

HOME Back to the ship, e.g. haul the anchor home.

LEEWARD, ALEE, or **LEE** The opposite of *weather*.
  In the lee of an object Sheltered from the wind by the object.

ONBOARD or **ABOARD** On or in the vessel.

OUTBOARD Outside the hull of the vessel but attached to it.

OVERBOARD Off the vessel and in the water.
  To go by the board To break loose and go overboard.
  Adrift Overboard, afloat, and free.

PORT To the left when facing forward.

STARBOARD To the right when facing forward.

STARBOARD or **PORT TACKS** Sailing with the wind coming over the starboard or portside of the vessel.

WEATHER The side of the vessel over which the wind is blowing.

GENERAL ORDERS TO THE CREW

BAIL Pump or scoop the water out of the boat.

CALL Summon, especially from below.

EASY Carefully.

GINGERLY Cautiously.

GIVE A HAND Help on this job.

Lend a hand (an order) A request for aid.

HANDLE HER Take charge of the boat.

HANDSOMELY Moderately and with care.
  Handsomely done In a shipshape manner.

LAY Go.

PIPE DOWN Be quiet.

SMARTLY Swiftly or daringly, and skillfully.

SPEAK or **HAIL** Call to a passing boat. (The customary hail is "Ahoy.")

STAND WATCH Go on duty.

STAND BY Await command

TUMBLE OUT (a) Get up and dressed; (b) Come on deck in a hurry.

TURN IN (a) Go to bed; (b) Go below.

TURN OUT Come on deck ready to work.

TURN TO Get to work.

ORDERS TO THE HELM

CONNING Giving detailed instructions, courses, or orders to the helm in a channel or in difficult waters.

NAVIGATING Directing the course of the vessel, especially doing so by plotting fixes and determining courses.

PILOTING Steering in or out of channels or harbors.

STEERING Handling the helm.

BEAR or **HEAD** Steer for the bearing or in the compass direction indicated.

BEAR UP, POINT UP or **HIGHER, LET HER UP,** or **HAUL THE WIND** Head more into the wind.
  Bear off, pay off or **let her off** Swing more down the wind.
  Ease her Relieve the strain on the vessel by pointing up more, even luffing slightly.
  Ease the rudder Reduce its angle.
  Fill away or **keep her full** Fill the sails by bearing more off the wind, especially after coming about or luffing.
  Keep her up Continue to sail close to the wind.
  Luff Point up until the sails spill the wind.
  Veer Alter course so as to head less into the wind.

BRING HER UP TO, or **ROUND TO** Point the vessel into the wind.
  Lie to Stop the vessel by heading into the wind and keeping her there or, when under bare poles, letting her seek her own heading.

COME ABOUT Shift tacks by heading into the wind.

FEEL YOUR WAY Maneuver cautiously, usually with the depthsounder going.

HARD ALEE Bring the vessel about by putting the helm down.

JIBE (as an order when running) Steer to leeward so as to fill the sails by the lee and ease them over to the other side.
  Wear (over) Change tacks when beating by turning down the wind and jibing.

PORT (or starboard) **YOUR HELM** Push the tiller to port (or starboard) and thus swing the ship to starboard (or port).
  Put your helm up (or **down**) Pull the tiller to windward (or push it to leeward). When the helm is *hard down* (i.e., as far down as possible), the rudder is *hard up.*
  Meet her When steering in a sea, reverse the rudder in advance so as to stop the the vessel just as it reaches its course.

STAND IN TOWARD, or **OUT FROM** Steer toward or away from a port, or other land.

STEADY, or **STEADY AS YOU GO** Hold your course.

TOUCH AT Stop at a port.

COMPASS AND WIND COURSES AND ALL BEARINGS MAY ALSO BE GIVEN AS ORDERS TO THE HELM, e.g., "bear northeast," "bear for the standpipe broad on the port bow."

ORDERS AS TO HANDLING RIGGING OR GEAR

GENERAL ORDERS

Avast or **so** Hold fast, stop where you are.

Break out any gear Get it out of stowage and, usually, ready for use.

House or **stow** (a) Put away in some receptacle where it is secure; (b) take rigging or sails in and put away permanently.

Make shipshape Put into perfect condition and order.

Overhaul Put in good order (applied to gear and to the contents of containers).

Secure Set some part of the rigging or some job in condition to leave it.

Snug down Get everything topsides secured with minimum windage, ready to ride out a storm.

Square away Get everything relating to a job completely ready for action, or completely done.

ORDERS AS TO STAYS

Ease a stay Loosen it.

Free a stay Cast it loose. It is applied especially to back stays. The hurried call is *Backstay away!*

Set up or **set up on** a stay Make it taut or tauter.

Trim a stay Make it the proper tautness.

ORDERS AS TO SAILS

Bend a sail Put it on its spars.

Unbend a sail Take it off its spars.

Furl a sail Secure it by rolling it up and lashing it with gaskets to its spar.

Skin (of a sail) The outside canvas of a furled sail.

Flake down a sail Secure it by lowering it in folds.

Loose a sail Unfurl it.

Hoist or **set** a sail Haul it into sailing position.

Break out a light sail or flag Set it so that it fills or flies suddenly.

Fly a flag or kite Hoist a flag to the breeze or set a light sail.

Lower, strike, or **take in** a sail or flag Bring it down. The hurried calls are *jib in, main in, lower away,* and *douse.*

Douse a sail Bring it down in a hurry.

Scandalize a sail Break the set of a sail so as to reduce its pull.

Shorten a sail or **reef** a sail Reduce the sail area.

Reef down Reef greatly.

Shake out a reef Remove the reef.

ORDERS AS TO RUNNING RIGGING

Cast off Free and let go.

Cast off or **let go a line** Free it and let it run.

Let go by the run Cast off and pay out the line (e.g., a sheet) in a hurry.

Pay out Let the line out under control.

Clear a line Free it from all impediments.

Coil down or **make up** a line Make it into a coil. Each turn of the coil is a fake.

Free a line Loosen it from its fastening or an impediment that holds it fast.

Hand taut As tight as can be pulled by hand without winches or other special tackle without swigging.

Haul a line Pull on it.

Haul home Pull it all the way in or until taut.

Heave a line Throw it.

Make a Flemish coil Coil in such a way that each *fake* is laid down on the deck forming a sort of mat.

Ballantine a coil Coil in three overlapping circles so that it will run out freely.

Capsize a coil Turn it over and lay it down with the bitter end underneath, so that it will run out freely.

Make fast Fasten the line or fasten with a line.

Belay Make the rope fast by cleating.

Hitch Make the rope fast to a spar, etc., with an overlay which binds.

Lash Make anything fast with a line and knot.

Overhaul a tackle Pull the line out through the block until ample slack is free; e.g., "overhaul the port backstay."

ORDERS AS TO HALYARDS

Set up on a halyard Tighten it.

(A halyard is *chock-a-block* when set up until its blocks touch.)

Slack a halyard Loosen it.

Swig Pull sideways or *sway* on a hand taut halyard to tighten it further.

ORDERS AS TO SHEETS (sometimes also spoken in terms of sails)

Closehaul Trim the sails as flat as possible and so that they will still draw well.

Flatten down Trim so that sails are flatter than before.

Pay out or slack Let out under control.

Slack away Pay out under control.

Start or *ease* Pay out a little so the sail is less flat.

Spill the wind or *luff* Slacken until the wind ceases wholly to fill the sail.

Sheet down Trim and belay, especially after coming about.

Trim Haul in a little so as to cause the sail to set properly.

ORDERS AS TO ROPE HANDLING

Fish Repair a broken spar by splinting it with wooden pieces (fishes) and seizing the junction.

Freshen Shift an anchor cable or running gear to change the place of wear.

Lace Thread through grommets.

Lay a rope Twist loose strands into a rope.
Lay of a rope The way the strands twist together.

Marry Sew two ropes together for temporary purposes, such as reeving them through a block.

Mouse Close the opening of a hook by seizing it with light cordage, or lash the pin of a shackle to prevent it unscrewing.

Parcel Wrap a rope in canvas to prevent chafing.

Reeve Thread through a block, fairlead, grommet, etc.
A rope *renders well* when, after reeving, it runs freely.

Seize Bind with a small rope or twine.

Serve Wrap with marline or twine.

Splice Join two ropes or make an eye in a rope, by interlacing the strands.

Trice down or **up** Hold down or lift up and lash.

Whip Serve a rope's end.

Worm Wind small stuff in the channel of the lay between the strands so as to make a smooth tubular surface for parceling.

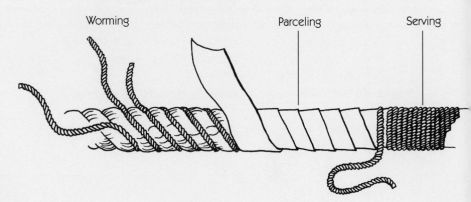

Worming   Parceling   Serving

ORDERS AS TO ENTERING HARBOR

SOUNDING
Call the lead State the depth found in fathoms.
Heave the lead Find the depth in fathoms (6 feet) by throwing out a lead line.

ANCHORING
Break out or **trip** the anchor Loosen it from the bottom so that it is *atrip* or has *broken ground* or is *broken out.*
Fish the anchor Catch the fluke of the anchor with a line while it is hanging from the bowsprit and make it fast to the bow, outboard.
Give scope or **pay out** the anchor cable Let out more.
Haul the anchor cockbill Haul it up to the bowsprit so that it is hanging free over the bows and above the water.
Haul the anchor short Pull in the anchor cable until the anchor is directly under the bow; i.e., the anchor rode is up and down, at *short stay.*
Heave on the anchor cable Pull in on it.
Let go the anchor (never "drop" the anchor) Release its cable and let it run out.
Sight the anchor Haul it to the surface to see if it is fouled.
Weigh the anchor Haul it up. When the anchor is off-bottom, it is *aweigh.*

MOORING
Cast off a mooring, or mooring buoy Free the vessel from the mooring.
Pick up a mooring, or mooring buoy Come to a stop at it and make fast to it.

THE MOORING OR PIER

Make Come to a stop at the mooring or pier.

To fetch short or *to fetch long* Errors in mooring.

Put out from or **push off** Leave the mooring or pier on a cruise or sail.

THE PIER

Bear away from a pier or vessel Move or steer away from it.

Cast off from a pier Release all ropes so that the boat is free.

Fend off or **shore off** from a pier or vessel Push away from it.

HANDLING THE DINGHY

Back water Work the oars in reverse.

Bend to your oars Pull hard.

Boat your oars Put them inside the boat.

Easy all Stop pulling.

Feather Flatten your oar blades while they are moving forward in the air, especially just letting them touch the water.

Give way or **pull away** Start rowing.

Rest on your oars Let the boat coast ahead with the oars broad off.

Row Pull on the oars.

Scull Make headway by a zigzag motion of a single oar astern.

Ship your oars Put them into the row locks.

Shove off Leave the pier or shore.

Stand by Get ready to start.

Way enough Stop rowing and get ready to boat your oars.

ORDERS AS TO HAULING OUT AND PUTTING IN

HAULING OUT
    Dismantle Take off all rigging and gear.
    Haul out Pull the boat out of water.
    Lay up Haul out for the winter.
    Shore up Brace the vessel upright with shores.

FITTING OUT
    Burn off Burn off the paint on the hull so as to get clean wood to paint on.
    Caulk the seams Drive cotton or oakum in the seams to prevent leaking.
    Cut in a boot top Paint a small band at the waterline.
    Pay the seams Fill them with putty.
    Rig the sails and lines Put them in working positions and order.
        Bend the sails Fasten them on their spars.
        Reeve the lines Draw them through their blocks and leaders.
    Rig the vessel Put all masts, stays, and running rigging in place.
    Step the mast Put the mast in place.
    Trim the stays Tighten the stays properly.

ALPHABETICAL INDEX
OF TERMS

69